Echoes Of The In-Between

Navigating Shadows and Light

Symone Platania

BookLeaf
Publishing

India | USA | UK

Dedication

To my younger brother and his wonderful wife, whose love and laughter remind me of the beauty found in life's uncertainties. To Cassie, my unwavering friend, whose support lights the path through the shadows. And to all those who navigate the in-between—may you find strength in your struggles and hope in every whisper of resilience.

Preface

In the delicate dance of emotions, we often find ourselves caught in the in-between—a space where joy and sorrow intertwine, where hope flickers amidst uncertainty. This collection of poems is a reflection of that journey, exploring the profound complexities of emotional instability while seeking the light that resides within the shadows.

Each poem is an echo of my own experiences and the stories of those around me. It is for anyone who has felt the weight of doubt yet yearns for solace.

These verses aim to resonate with the struggles and triumphs we all face, offering a gentle reminder that even in our darkest moments, hope can blossom like a wildflower through cracks in the pavement. I invite you to journey with me through these pages, to embrace the chaos, and to discover the beauty that lies in the in-between.

Acknowledgements

As I reflect on the creation of this collection, I am filled with gratitude for those who have walked alongside me in this journey.

To my family, thank you for your patience and understanding during the countless times I have spent lost in far away places. Your love and unwavering support has been my greatest inspiration.

To my dear friends, your shared moments of silence, comfort, and joy have shaped my perspective and enriched my poetry. I am grateful for your presence in my life.

Lastly, a heartfelt thanks to the readers who find resonance in these pages: thank you for inviting my words into your lives. Your connection to my poetry is a gift I cherish.

The Path

There is no rest
for the tired, wandering soul;
filled with exhaustion,
left to bare the weight
that presses down,
giving no respite.

The gate to both worlds
stays as a luminous presence,
sucking you in,
confusing you more.
The roads branch out—
many possibilities,
some converging,
others spreading further out.

One must be wary,
not hastily choosing
that which appears simple,
for these easy choices
can lead to a more complicated ending,
one where pain becomes overwhelming
and difficult to bear.

Rise up and push through,
for beauty emerges
only after the storm.
Make the difficult choices first,
pushing harder
and going further
than you ever thought possible.

Drifting

Sometimes the distance seems so vast. . .
I ponder with many thoughts, wishing to be free. . .
empty
In that wish though, a disconnect may grow. . .
Just drifting through the motions, void of feeling. . .

Floating between the delicate paths of life and death. . .
The weight that keeps me from moving eventually will
disappear. . .an echo
A new weightlessness that can now open itself to the
possibilities. . .
A courage to go forward and forge a new way. . .

Broken

I am broken.

So many words unspoken.
If let out to be heard
Rebuke will meet it and then I feel absurd.
The pieces of my heart are scattered;
And what's left of my soul too feels like it will soon
shatter.

Clear salted drops push themselves out now;
Falling wherever comfort shows a helping hand
But then it all feels like quicksand.
Sinking so fast under;
With nothing to grab so my body shivers and shudders

Hoping in the end
Fate will be kind;
Bring me back to reality
and heal my mind.

'Cause I am broken.

Strength

A stark fading light beats within,
Slowly darkened by the self-made sin.
Melting away the essence of my being,
Making whole again what was lost -- changing and renewing.
A hardened path laid out before me; one I must tread.
Even deep down with anxiousness growing will I still head.
Because in the end I will be stronger for it,
Opening up to the better moments and cherishing them more;
And finally the peaceful bliss will be evermore.

Out of the Void

From the void I emerge...
Searching and looking within others' eyes.
Something I can build my belief on, ignoring the internal
cries.

I do this often and yet, I am constantly drawn back in
Escaping the mold that grows and festers in the deepest
recesses of my mind.
Is a hard task, growing even more too I find.

Tomorrow will be the same.
All I have is that faint glimmer given by life's precious
grace.
To find rest and peace in a shared souls embrace.

A Deep Yearning

Shh... don't speak and waste precious breaths on wasted ears.
My soul has felt your sorrow as the winds are felt through the trees.
A gentle hum of winged voices seeping into the inner threads of my being.

Your golden tears shall know the comforts of secrets forgotten.
For chained are we in the torments but stronger will we become.
A prayer of hope lingering on parted lips.

Dark will meet light and unshackled chains will stay as a faint reminder,
of the long and lonely prison.
Faith and Hope in that tomorrow has made the gates of love open,
to what was in the beginning and will be in the End...

Cultivated

Like a flower, if not cultivated or cared for;
We too can wither and die on the cold bare floor.
But sometimes the moods of the seasons,
Are just cycles we must go through for each their own reason.
Flowers have life, death, and rebirth,
We also as we go through life too unearth,
The secrets from when we rise and fall and rise again.
As long as we learn from each experience in which to attain,
A growth and prosperity that enriches the soul in the end.

Dare to Be

In the heart of the day,
There is always much to say.
To the world, to ourselves;
Our mind never stops being self-aware.

The question is...
...do we even care.
To look beyond us and just...
...Dare

Dare to be bold,
Dare to be kind,
Dare to not fold,
Dare to even shine.

Dare to show you care,
In a world where caring is a crime.

String of Fate

Your hand reached out,
As did mine.
A Spring encounter,
Connecting us through time.

The faint rains of seasons pass,
Washing away a destined path;
Once crossed but never trodden.
There lays Sorrow's Garden.

Faint and Unbeknownst,
Two bound blossoming souls.
This intertwining weave of the red string of Fate,
It's enchanted and melodic instrument shows;

A delicate story,
Needing nurture and glory.
For only the truth-seekers know,
That in it, true love will grow.

Standing Strong

Breathing high when we sink so low,
Drinking it all in just for show;
Just bending our knee to the crowd,
Facing life that won't let us out;
Try to find what was lost and make it found.

Hoping for a better tomorrow,
As my world is turned upside down and left in sorrow;
I drag my feet and lift my aching bones,
Crashing about and stumbling through,
As disheartened hearts go, from the tragedy of fake
news.

Fighting when fighting is a necessary play,
When words long used no longer have any say;
I will then take up a stand,
And perhaps hope will prevail for the Truest Good,
Making free what never truly was understood.

The Fade

I am consumed by the many thoughts that fill my mind...
Soon I will fade into the nothingness.
I am diminished skin cell by skin cell,
Till the only thing left is the emptiness.
In flight will I soar through the spaces of the in-between,
Filling the void unseen.
I'll be nothing more than a faint memory...
A picture on a wall,
A face on a screen;
And in time, I will be nothing.
Not the voices in your dream beckoning,
Nor the hand in the darkness calling.
I am the Fade...

Blind

I blindly stare towards your unknown gaze;
Wondering about were thoughts lay
 and your mind roams.

I wait for your eyes to meet mine.
To communicate beyond the words
and only listen to the sublime of our hearts,
Connected as one.

Release

I breathe deeply
Then release above to thee.
A messenger, a warrior,
I will take you on your life further.
Breathe deeply...
Then live.

You let go before I even could grab a hold of you.
What am I to do
As I also am soon to fade.
We are heading our separate ways;
Each in a different direction,
Chosen by the more difficult path.

We suffer in silence
becoming more.
We take flight towards the high heavens
releasing our bondage.
That which was holding us down,
has now given us wings to fly.

All the Faces

All the faces of you,
all the faces of you,
Just seem to come out on cue.
Some bold, some shy, some hopeful,
Scared, tired, fake, brave, lonely,
or misunderstood.
I'm sure deep down you would
lessen the complication and confusion if you could.

So...breathe easy for a little,
breathe easy for a little,
breathe easy for a little while.
No need to overwhelm,
no need to suffocate;
All you need to do,
is just take time to dedicate;
and help yourself decimate.

All the fears, all the worries, all the pain.
All those pointless thoughts
that take over your brain.
Your faces are part of you;
Just don't keep thinking you have to choose.
'Cause, you are who you are when you just meditate,

and then gravitate to
to be the best of you

Puppet on a String

With strings I am pulled,
I am controlled.
I am a puppet on a string,
trying to loosen its hold

In the tears that ebb away at my soul,
They externalize into a flow,
Glistening in unhealthy colors
glittering cold

Seeping down my face into the unknown,
Wishes like dreams may reap what they sow.
There I am, a puppet on a string,
Trying to loosen its hold.

Angel

Breathing in with a deepened sigh,
Trying to let go of all the regrets that have passed me on
by.
Tears flow for the pain and hurt.
But you give me strength and all of your support.
You are the angel in the distance,
Whispering courage for my resistance.

Fluttering Companion

The lonely soul beckons,
In search of companionship.
Even when shrinking within itself;
It yearns for connection.

Succumbed to mere micro atoms of thought,
Which swirl in chaotic congruence.
In the bright light of day;
Will another soul connect.

Hidden as a symbol of harmony,
Fluttering at the shoulder
A sweat rhythm in my ear,
Whistling an ethereal tune.

Removed

Another day to have been broken,
Beyond a point of extreme.
There in the cold emptiness,
Or the heated furry of rage that comes,
Eating away at the inner core,
Where thoughts become intertwined with darkness,
Not knowing which right way to turn.

The mind is looking for an out.
A way to get away from the pain
That permeates across all the inner workings of the
body's will.
Hitting all at once,
deafening it's control.
The mask that was,
is now removed.

Laying bare what wants to be hidden,
Yes, I am broken.
Now I must seek out
the sweet fragrance of hope that can pull me up
Away from the shackled
and putridness placed in my path;
So that I may be broken no more.

Breathing for One Day

Breathing in
breathing out.
Giving up
fading out.

Wishing for more
but passing to the floor.

Walking in
walking out.
Passing by
wishing to fly;

and stay missing.

Curled into a corner
looking like a loner.
It won't be much longer
I know I will be stronger.

...One Day

After many of them have I prayed.
Hoped and hoped and hoped

but still delayed
...Yes to one day.

Echoes Calling

Do you hear the echoes that will break me in the night.
It calls me forward, praying on all my fears.
Drawing me out and imprisoning my mind.
A messenger comes in the hidden light
within the darkness that is surrounding and choking me
down.
There is a hunger that is ever present and never seeming
to be satisfied.
A sound in the distance is knocking.
I believe that it is a dream calling,
Calling me back into the deep sleep
that I have awoken from.
Yes, it is calling, calling.

Caged Shadows

Like shadows in a cage,
Not knowing if it is them to which we are afraid.
Given that not much attention is there placed.
Soon we will see it as our own survival that is in a race.

Oh shadow in the cage.
Why is it too late that I have chosen to be afraid;
Afraid of you a shadow hiding in the cage.

Soon my senses will darken,
Darken by that which is unbidden.
By a shadow no longer in its cage
Coming at me with unprecedented rage.

Now it is I that must hide in its cage;
To face an era of a new age.
Or to find my place within a new page.

One which I have written
To have a life that is worth livin'
I take up what's left of my courage;
Treating my mind as something that can be foraged.

In the end I will come out winning.

So in this end is my beginning.
A new way to start living.

Now go back oh shadow
To live forever in a new cage
To trap forever that unwanted rage
My dearest shadow back in its cage.

I have grown strong in your removal
and it has given life to me that is crucial
Thank you my shadow in a cage, placing my hope in
renewal.

The Crow's Road

Dark restless soul
haunted in the night by a possessed crow.
Perched in the ancient tree at the end of the road.

I hear its unwanted whisper,
Like an echo in the night
I glance at that candlelight window and wonder at the
sight

Deep in the piercing crow's eyes
I see a scene play out of a horrific demise
Startled, I back away from death's play

I then sit by the fireside
Pondering if this is how I die
But within moments that felt like hours,

I take up my watch there and then
Seizing the stark white reflection that cowers when eyes
have locked again.
Upon the crow at the road's end.

Will fates allow that destiny be given a bend.
Something from which I can defend.

Toward a path safe from Death's wanting grasp.

I wake
Yes, yes, it very will perhaps.

www.ingramcontent.com/pod-product-compliance
Lightning Source LLC
LaVergne TN
LVHW021330200726